Spiritual Guidance: Trusting the Voice Within

A workbook to enhance your spiritual wisdom

*Dr. Kimberly K. Friedman
and Lisa Miliaresis*

BALBOA
PRESS
A DIVISION OF HAY HOUSE

Copyright © 2013 Dr. Kimberly K. Friedman and Lisa Miliaresis.

All rights reserved. No part of this book may be used or reproduced by any means, graphic, electronic, or mechanical, including photocopying, recording, taping or by any information storage retrieval system without the written permission of the publisher except in the case of brief quotations embodied in critical articles and reviews.

Balboa Press books may be ordered through booksellers or by contacting:

Balboa Press
A Division of Hay House
1663 Liberty Drive
Bloomington, IN 47403
www.balboapress.com
1-(877) 407-4847

Because of the dynamic nature of the Internet, any web addresses or links contained in this book may have changed since publication and may no longer be valid. The views expressed in this work are solely those of the author and do not necessarily reflect the views of the publisher, and the publisher hereby disclaims any responsibility for them.

The author of this book does not dispense medical advice or prescribe the use of any technique as a form of treatment for physical, emotional, or medical problems without the advice of a physician, either directly or indirectly. The intent of the author is only to offer information of a general nature to help you in your quest for emotional and spiritual well-being. In the event you use any of the information in this book for yourself, which is your constitutional right, the author and the publisher assume no responsibility for your actions.

Any people depicted in stock imagery provided by Thinkstock are models, and such images are being used for illustrative purposes only. Certain stock imagery © Thinkstock.

Printed in the United States of America.

ISBN: 978-1-4525-7519-3 (sc)
ISBN: 978-1-4525-7520-9 (e)

Library of Congress Control Number: 2013909685

Balboa Press rev. date: 7/11/2013

Prologue

It is a secret of the world that all things subsist and do not die, but only retire a little from sight and afterwards return again. Nothing is dead; men feign themselves as dead, and endure mock funerals and mournful obituaries, and there they stand looking out of the window, sound and well, in some strange new disguise.

– Ralph Waldo Emerson

Our human existence is like a school. We are here to learn. Regardless of what grade you are in, what curriculum you are studying, and with whom you have chosen to study; we hope that this book will assist you on your personal journey.

We begin with the premise that we are all spiritual beings having a human experience. This isn't a religious text, but instead a spiritual workbook. We purposefully wrote this book in a conversational tone - a book that you can pick up and feel as though you are talking with a friend. We will use terms like intuition, spirituality, universe, God, infinite intelligence, spiritual guidance, white light, angels, prayer, souls, channeling, reincarnation, and karma. We know that some terms may seem more familiar to you than others. If a particular term does not resonate with you, feel free to substitute a term that is more comfortable for your belief system. There are many paths towards spirituality, enhanced awareness, and self-realization. We feel that people of all backgrounds, religions, and spiritual belief systems can find something of value within these pages.

It is our hope that the exercises discussed in this book will allow you to reconnect with your innate wisdom that sometimes gets covered up during our busy lives. We hope to promote an understanding that there is a higher guidance, healing energy, and insight available to each and every one of us simply for the asking.

We have written this workbook for people of all ages. It can be used individually or in a group setting. We welcome families to perform these exercises together and enjoy the shared awakening. Although we recommend that you initially read through the chapters and exercises from beginning to end, we invite you to follow your intuition and revisit certain passages as you feel directed to do so. These practices do not need to be performed in any specific order, at any specific time, or in any specific place. Just as our own spiritual awakening does not work via a calendar or rule book, there is no schedule or regulations associated with this book. We hope that you can incorporate these exercises into your day-to-day lives in order to become more conscious of the special moments that occur around us each and every day.

Before you begin, we have one, and only one, "rule": you must begin from a place without judgment or competition. In order to get into a relaxed frame of mind and open yourself up to all possibilities, we suggest you listen to a complimentary guided meditation provided for our readers at www.2communicate.net. You cannot be too advanced or too inexperienced for this book; even the simplest exercise can be magical if you allow. Give yourself permission to just have fun as you move through this practice and release any pressure on yourself to yield any particular outcome. Now, just relax, take off your shoes, let go of any little preoccupations that you may have collected during the day, take a deep breath, and let's begin!

Nothing in this workbook is intended to be medical advice or a substitute for medical care. It is not intended to diagnose, treat, cure or prevent any disease.

Table of Contents

Chapter 1	**What Are You Seeking?**	**1**
Chapter 2	**Everything Is Energy**	**4**
	Energy Awareness Exercise #1	7
	Energy Awareness Exercise #2	9
	Energy Awareness Exercise #3	11
	Energy Awareness Exercise #4	12
Chapter 3	**Law of Attraction**	**20**
	Exercise #1: Use the Law of Attraction in Your Day to Day Life	22
	Exercise #2: Mindful Observation	24
	Exercise #3: Creating for Others	26
	Exercise #4: Positive Affirmations	26
	Exercise #5: Journaling—the Quick and Easy Way!	27
Chapter 4	**Maintenance**	**29**
	Energy Cleaning Tool Box - Exercises #1-12	31
Chapter 5	**Balance**	**35**
Chapter 6	**Nourish Yourself**	**41**
	Exercise #1: Mindful Eating	44
	Exercise #2: Nourish the Physical	48

	Exercise #3: Nourish the Physical (2)	48
	Exercise #4: Nourish the Mind	49
	Exercise #5: Nourish the Energy and Spirit	49
Chapter 7	**Ethics**	**51**
Chapter 8	**Connecting the Dots**	**58**
	Exercise #1: Breath of Appreciation	62
	Exercise #2: Choose a Shift	62
	Exercise #3: Detach from Drama	63

Chapter 1

What Are You Seeking?

*There Is A Voice Inside Of You
That Whispers All Day Long,
I Feel That This Is Right For Me,
I Know That This Is Wrong.
No Teacher, Preacher, Parent, Friend
Or Wise Man Can Decide
What's Right For You- Just Listen To
The Voice That Speaks Inside.*
- Shel Silverstein, American Poet,
September 1930 – May 1999

Let us introduce ourselves…Lisa Miliaresis, psychic medium, and Dr. Kimberly Friedman, past life regression counselor and yoga teacher. Writing this workbook was probably the last thing we thought we would be doing. We are busy moms who work full time and enjoy very rich, full lives. Yet we both seek answers to age-old questions about why we are here, what it all means, what happens after death and before birth, and how our lives are interconnected. And, through many years of personal practice and workshops, we know that our questions may not be that different than yours. So, we begin with a question, "What are you seeking?"

Some may be looking for validation and understanding that our lives are eternal. Some may be searching for the healing that can be found in knowing that our loved ones on the other side can hear our thoughts and prayers. Some may desire to release stuck patterns or emotions that seem to be recurrent within their lives. Some may wish to improve their financial or emotional or physical well being. Some may wish to explore that age-old question of, "Is this life all that there is?" Some may be looking to enhance their ability to receive and interpret the symbolic language that mediums use when communicating with those that have crossed over from this lifetime. Some don't exactly know why they search for personal growth and knowledge, it is just a natural part of who they are and why they are here without entirely possessing the words to explain it.

So what are you seeking? Do you want to enhance your ability to live a life with more joy and ease?

In our experience, enhancing your spiritual awareness can allow you to:

- Guide your thoughts to form positive life experiences
- Communicate with loved ones who have crossed over
- Tap into the potential of healing energies such as reiki

- Identify angels or guides that are available to assist you in this lifetime
- Release repeated patterns, blocked energy, or troubled emotions
- Deeply understand your true identity as a loving and peaceful spiritual being
- And, get a few more giggles and enjoyment out of life!

You are already seeking a deeper connection to spiritual guidance just by the very nature of the fact that you are holding this book. You chose Earth to serve as your school and you established lessons to be learned and connections to others before you arrived. But, once you got here, it became your free will to choose your pathways in this lifetime. This book is possibly one of those pathway choices for you.

Throughout the following chapters, we will discuss ways to enhance your awareness of the energy and guidance systems within and around you at all times. This awareness will allow you to feel your senses on a whole new level as well as find senses you didn't even know you had. We will also discuss the importance of maintaining the physical, mental, energetic and spiritual bodies. Many of the suggested tools are available to each and every one of us without cost or any special equipment or space. You only need the desire and the commitment to fine-tune and enhance a connection to your own personal spirituality while you allow the unfolding to occur. Congratulations on making the commitment toward personal growth and beginning to uncover what you are seeking.

Chapter 2

Everything Is Energy

Energy is abundant and each of us is able to tap into this abundant flow of love at all times. This flow is unconditional loving energy from a source of love and light.
— Lisa Miliaresis, From Meditation

Everything is energy. People, animals, trees, the Earth, water, desks, even this book-they are all energy. Science classes teach us that neutrons, protons and electrons vibrate at specific wavelengths or frequencies to produce everything we can touch, taste, see, hear, or feel.

But does energy only create objects that we can identify with our basic senses? Energy might not take a physical form. For example, visible light is energy of a vibration level detectable to the human eye, but ultraviolet or infrared light exists even though we can't see it with our eyes. Sound waves are another type of energy. However, there are some sound vibrations, like those emitted from a dog whistle, that are not perceptible to the human ear. Just because we can't recognize something with our physical senses, doesn't mean it is nonexistent. It is actually helpful that our human bodies can't perceive all the energy around us. Can you imagine what it would be like if we noticed all the cell phone transmissions, radio waves, and satellite transmissions that surround us? We really wouldn't want our energy receivers to become **that** sensitive.

Energy is all around us; it is in the air we breathe. We can sense it, if we pay attention. For example, if you walk into a room where others were just fighting, you can sense the tension in the air. It feels thick and angry and uncomfortable. The saying "you can cut the tension with a knife" comes from that energetic awareness.

How about the energy you sense when you meet someone for the first time and you feel an instant connection. Or, an instant repulsion. You may be responding to a visual characteristic or a verbal interaction, but you may be responding to an energetic interaction as well. Energy influences us, subconsciously guides our actions and reactions; and, if we become more aware of its presence, can assist us as we travel through our lessons in life.

Everyone has the ability to become more sensitive to the energy around us. We all have natural instincts and awareness. However, over time, we begin to assume that our gut instincts that develop from energetic pulls are just silly. When that little voice inside tells us to beware of something, we are able to dismiss it as just overreacting. We chalk things up to coincidence instead of something more. Our energetic awareness gets suppressed, or a little dormant, until we start to rediscover and trust it.

So let's start with the energy found within our physical bodies. The human body has an obvious physical matter, but it also has an energetic existence that is beyond that which is easily seen with the eyes or felt with the hands. The energy body is sometimes referred to as an "aura" and it extends both internally and externally. It interacts with everything around us and can actually be photographed through Kirlian photography. There is even thought that the "halos" that one often sees depicted around angels or religious figures is a representation of that aura. But auras aren't only for angels or religious leaders, we all have energy around and within us.

Many different schools of thought will label body energy differently. You may see terms such as chi or ki or prana or manna or life force or biomagnetic energy – all different terms from various modalities which define the energy that flows within and around us. There are different healing therapies that work with energy such as Reiki, Acupuncture, Healing Touch, Body Reactivation, Shiatsu, and others. Some mainstream hospitals are even beginning to use energy therapies as an adjunct to traditional Western medical care, and medical schools are beginning to teach "integrative" or "alternative" medicine techniques. But, for the purposes of this workbook, the labels or specific terminology aren't that important - enhancing an awareness of that energy is the intent - not which label you choose to apply to that energy.

So let's start with a simple energy awareness exercise.

Energy Awareness Exercise #1

In this exercise you will experience your own energy by creating a pull between your hands. Sit in a relaxed but upright position with your feet flat on the floor. Begin to breathe deeply and rhythmically through your nose. Allow your eyelids to close gently for a few breaths. Begin to lengthen out your inhales and your exhales. Maybe even pause for just a few moments between each inhale and exhale to sink into that momentary stillness. Allow yourself to begin to relax and let go. Permit your shoulders to release down the back creating a little extra space between your shoulders and your ears and release any tension that you may have developed during the responsibilities of your life today. Gently float your eyelids open and you are ready to begin.

1. Hold your hands together in front of your stomach area.
2. Turn your hands so that the palms are facing each other and hold the hands about 6 inches apart.
3. Continue to take slow deep breaths – attempt to lengthen out your exhales so they're just as long, if not longer, than your inhales.
4. On the next inhalation breath, slowly move your hands away from each other to about 12 inches apart. Hold for a count of three and then slowly bring your hands together until you feel a slight

resistance between your palms. You can allow your hands to move out and in until you begin to develop this awareness of the resistance, or energy, between your palms. It might feel a little silly--as though you're playing an invisible accordion.

5. Repeat this process several times. Try moving your hands slowly with the rhythm of your breath. See if you can become aware of the energy between the two hands.

   You may feel this energy more as the hands approach close to each other, but with practice you may be able to feel this energy even when your hands are further apart. It might be helpful to keep your eyes closed so that your vision does not distract you from the feeling. Sometimes people will get the sense that this energy feels just like two magnets being drawn together. Some people will feel it more like opposite ends of a magnet facing each other and the energy is repelling. Either way is perfect and neither is right or wrong.

6. Once you are aware this energy, you can slowly move your hands in a circular motion. Notice if you feel the energy change in its vibration or intensity as you begin to move your hands. Some may feel a "prickly" sensation in their palms, a tingling sensation, a warm sensation, while others claim to be playing with an energy ball.

Energy Awareness Exercise #2

In a seated position with your feet flat on the floor, begin to breathe deeply in and out through your nose. Stack your vertebrae one on top of the other, growing tall through the spine, allow your shoulders to release down, and settle in. Always take a few moments to simply relax before beginning an exercise.

1. Hold your left hand in front of your stomach area with the palm facing to the right.
2. Take your index and middle finger on your right hand and extend them long while curling in your thumb, ring finger, and pinky finger together-just like you are pointing with your index and middle finger.
3. Point your index finger and middle finger towards the palm of your left hand holding the fingers about 1 ½ to 2 inches off the left palm.
4. Begin to make a small circle with the fingers of your right hand. It might be helpful to again close your eyes so as to not let the vision interfere with your perception of the energy.
5. Continue to draw a circle in the air with your right fingers while maintaining awareness of what you might feel in the left palm.
6. Once you feel a circular motion to the energy tracing along the left palm, notice what happens if you reverse the direction of the circle. Do not attach to any result or feel disappointment, as each of these exercises will be a different experience

for each individual. Allow yourself to experience these exercises with a sense of light play, remembering that there is no right or wrong.
7. Now try moving your hands further apart to see if you can still feel the energy movement with more distance between the hands.

After you begin to develop an awareness of the energy that you possess within your body, the next step is to become aware of the energy beyond your physical body.

We have all probably seen Einstein's mass energy equivalence formula that states $E=mc^2$. What does this formula say? The scientific amongst us would say energy equals mass times the speed of light squared. But what does this formula really mean to us? Although this formula was used to illustrate that we can break down material mass to form energy such as is the case with an atomic bomb, this formula can also be used to express the premise that the building block of everything within our material world is energy. There is energy in all the objects that you see around you. There is energy within your physical body which we explored in the first two exercises. But more importantly, there is unseen energy surrounding us as well. Further, our energy interacts with and influences the energy around us and the energy around us interacts with and influences us!

Let's expand those energy receptors to become more aware of energy in general. You have probably felt the energy of other people before, but you may not have been aware that you were doing so. Let's try another exercise.

Energy Awareness Exercise #3

You will need a partner for this exercise.

1. Have a friend sit down in front of you, facing away from you. (You can even do this with a pet if a human friend isn't available.)
2. Take the palms of your hands and rub them together rapidly building up a bit of heat between your palms.
3. Place your hands about three or 4 inches above the upper back of your partner.
4. Be patient and breathe deeply in and out through the nose. Feel free to float your eyes gently closed as that might help you increase your energy awareness.
5. Sense how the energy feels. You may pick up areas of heat, tingling, pulsing, coolness, a prickly sensation, or maybe something else. Gently move your hands about 4 inches above the surface of your partner's back and notice if the sensation changes in different areas as you move your hands. Notice if you feel the sensations more in one hand or the other.
6. Sometime your hands may feel as though they're being guided to one particular area or your intuition might suggest that your hands should linger in one particular place.

Often the sensations will become more obvious to you in time. You can even do this scanning technique with other objects as well, remembering that everything is energy. Try scanning the energy of a tree, other people, animals, your legs, even feel the energy rising off the hot pavement on a sunny summer day. You can scan and become aware of energy through practice with all kinds of animate or inanimate objects. Just like increasing the strength of a human muscle with repeated physical exercise, your abilities with energy awareness will improve with practice as well.

Energy Awareness Exercise #4

Psychometry can be a fun way to explore the energy inherent in objects. In fact, we find that it is often one of the highlights of the seminars that we conduct, and people are often amazed by what they can do when experimenting with psychometry.

Psychometry comes from the principal that an object has an energy field and that we have the ability to tap into that energy field and discover information about that object's history. Although it may sound like something from a bad psychic stage act, people are surprised over and over again as to how accurate their readings can actually be. So enter this exercise with a particularly open mind. Release any judgment and just allow yourself to have fun with it. It is best to perform this exercise with a partner. If it's possible, do this exercise with someone that you don't know very well. We know that might push you a little out of your comfort zone, but sometimes that is a good thing.

1. You will need a piece of paper, and a pen or pencil, and one object from each participant which has some level of significance to the participant. For example, you might choose a piece of jewelry that you frequently wear or an item that holds personal significance to you. It is important that your partner knows nothing about this particular item.
2. Choose one person to be the "reader" first and the other person to be the "recorder" first.
3. The reader will hold the object from the recorder in his or her hand.
4. The reader may wish to gently float his eyelids closed, breathe deeply and rhythmically, and focus on the object. The reader will then state anything that he feels, sees, hears, smells, tastes, or senses. It could be random thoughts or images, it could be a story or scenario, it could be colors, feelings, or something completely different. There is no right or wrong. There are no rules to how this progresses.
5. The recorder will simply write down anything that the person reading the object says. Resist the temptation to validate anything the person reading the object states. Do not feed any information. Do not shake your head yes or no. Try not to give the reader information through body language, subtle smiles, or other facial expressions. Be open and supportive because often the person reading the object may feel self-conscious or full of doubt. If needed, encourage the person reading the object by simply stating things like, "that's fine", "keep going", "it's okay".

6. After about 5 minutes or longer depending upon when the reader has completed his statements, return the object back to the recorder. (Be sure to allow enough time for the reader to express all of his thoughts, feelings, and images. It's okay for there to be pauses or silence between statements.)
7. After the reader has returned the object, the recorder will then tell the reader about the object. Often the reader will be surprised that the information that they received is accurate.
8. Now change roles and repeat with the second object.

No matter how many times we conduct psychometry experiments in our seminars, we consistently find that people are much better at this experiment than they anticipate that they will be. And, just like any other of the exercises in this workbook, the results seem to get better and better with practice.

We need to discover one final aspect about energy before moving forward. We now understand that our physical bodies contain an energetic identity. We also understand that all matter- all objects animate or inanimate- are composed of energy. Further, we understand that we are able to fine tune or exercise our energy receivers within our bodies to become more aware of the energy within and around us. But is there a way that we actually create energy?

The human body is regulated by the brain. The brain is

an incredible "computer system" responsible for thoughts, emotions, physical well being, voluntary and involuntary responses. It controls our ability to breathe, to provide nutrients to our body, to regulate our temperature, to protect us from threats, to think, to react, to exist. It allows us to live in physical form. But how does our brain do this?

Our brain analyzes energetic input and generates appropriate energetic responses via nerve impulses. It is a complex circuit of neurologic tissue which utilizes energy impulses to communicate. The energy found within the brain can be measured with medical recording devices such as an EEG. It is this ENERGY within the brain that creates our intelligence. This energy creates our emotions. This energy creates our survival instincts. This energy allows our bodies to coordinate complex movements throughout the day. This energy allows us to think. OUR THOUGHTS ARE ENERGY.

Until this point, everything we have stated would probably be supported, at least in some level, scientifically. Now we may reach a point of divergence in opinions. Some will look at the statement that our thoughts are energy and will extrapolate further from that and some will not. Just play along to see how it resonates with you.

Remember Einstein's mass equivalence theory, $E=mc^2$? Energy is equivalent to mass times the speed of light squared. Let's put that in simpler terms - energy equals physical matter influenced by the speed of light or, even simpler, energy equals "physical stuff". We know thoughts are energy. Do our thoughts actually have the power to create or manifest "stuff" as well? There are a plethora of self help books, movies, and motivational speakers that profess this very point - energy (in this case thoughts) can create or manifest outcomes. So if we become more aware of our own energy and how to work within our energetic systems, can we create desired outcomes in our own lives?

Let's take prayer for example. Prayer is simply thoughts organized and presented according to a religious or spiritual belief system. Some will say prayers according to the rituals of a particular church organization, some will say prayers without any particular religious affiliation, some will simply send out "good vibes" without labeling them as a prayer, and some will send out wishes. In the many years of work that Lisa has done as a psychic medium, one thing is abundantly clear. Our prayers are heard. Time and time again, Lisa will receive information during a channeling session which reveals something that a client had been praying about. Very often that client has told no one about those prayers.

There are so many examples of spirit hearing our prayers that it was challenging to just find a few. We decided to write about two very special examples.

Pets Are Beautiful Souls & Hear Our Thoughts & Prayers
In Lisa's words

My friend and coworker Diane called very upset because their pet rat "Butterscotch" ("Butters" for short) passed away. She was saddened to lose their pet, but even more upset because her son was so devastated. Diane tried her best to console her son, but he was quite upset. I suggested that he say a prayer to Butters asking her to give him some sort of sign so he knew she was okay. Later that day, he prayed and asked that Butterscotch come to him in a way that only he would know it was her. (We had no idea of what that "way" would be!)

A few days later, Diane and her son were upstairs. No one else was home. She heard some noise coming from downstairs and asked, "What is that I'm hearing"? He replied, "It's my iPod playing". They were not near the iPod nor had either of them turned it on; it started playing by itself. Diane jokingly said, "It's probably Butters" and chuckled! Very shortly after Diane made that joke, the iPod then turned off by itself. She then went downstairs to check the iPod and it was in the OFF/Locked position and no alarm or reminder had been set.

Diane went back upstairs to share this information with her son, actually wondering if her joke about Butters had some truth to it! Her son smiled and continued to play his Xbox Live. A few moments later he shouted, "Mom, look!" as he pointed to his TV - BUTTERS 1996 just logged onto the system to play!

First the iPod; then his Xbox Live! This is one clever rat - letting him know that she was okay by giving him a sign that was personal to him - just as he had ask for in his prayers!

Lisa's prayer is heard
in Lisa's words

June was a dear friend of the family who had always been a strong woman; she and my mother were divorcés at a time when it was not common to be a divorced woman with children. Our families spent many holidays together, and she loved me as if I were her own. We were a non-biological extended family. Shortly after I married and moved away from home, June transitioned suddenly from a fatal stroke.

After I had moved away, I met another woman named Barbara. We commuted back and forth from New Jersey to Philadelphia every day on the bus. She was very kind and took me under her wing. As a young married woman who had moved away from her family, I quickly began to feel like Barbara was family.

Barbara was a breast cancer survivor who was full of life. She had a lovely daughter from her first marriage, and she and her second husband had just adopted another child. One year later her cancer came back, fast and furious. Barbara tried to fight the cancer with everything from chemotherapy to a macrobiotic diet, but it was too late.

Time passed and Barbara was in the final stages of this lifetime and was bedridden in the hospital. Although I am comfortable with the life and death process, I do not like hospitals and I have a hard time visiting those who are ill. I knew Barbara was not going to live much longer, and I was trying to prepare myself for the next day when I was going to the hospital to visit my dying friend.

I prayed that night before I went to the hospital. I did not ask God to heal her illness for I knew her illness was terminal. Instead, I asked God to protect and love her. I also asked June, who I knew to be strong and loving, to go to Barbara and help her into the light where she could rest in peace with God. Remember that June and Barbara never knew each other in life. After praying and asking

June to help Barbara, I closed my eyes and saw what looked like a deformed image of Barbara. Her nose was narrow, face drawn, and her fingers were skeletal.

The next day I went to the hospital where I found Barbara, her husband and her daughter. Barbara looked just like my vision from the night before. Although it was difficult to see what her physical appearance had become, I was grateful I had seen her image prior to my visit so I did not react in shock. I released my anxiety and concentrated on only Barbara as she was in bed, heavily sedated, and clearly in the final stages of life. She was unconscious and unresponsive.

All of a sudden, Barbara sat up in her bed and looked at me. She clearly said, "June is here." and then plopped back in her bed, eyes closed, and unresponsive again. I was amazed! This was proof that my prayers were heard, and I knew Barbara would make it into the light just fine. Soon after, I went for coffee with Barbara's daughter and husband and told them of my prayer the night before. I asked if they or Barbara knew of anyone with the name June. They both said no. This was something I will never forget and June and Barbara will always be in my prayers.

Chapter 3

Law of Attraction

Each and every component that makes up your life experience is drawn to you by the powerful Law of Attraction's response to the thoughts you think and the story you tell about your life. Your money and financial assets; your body's state of wellness, clarity, flexibility, size, and shape; your work environment, how you are treated, work satisfaction, and rewards—indeed, the very happiness of your life experience in general—is all happening because of the story that you tell.

- Abraham, Excerpted from Money and the Law of Attraction — 3/31/09

People talk about the "Law of Attraction". You hear it mentioned on television, talk shows, books, and even blockbuster movies. Yet, what does it really mean?

The basic premise of the Law of Attraction is that "like attracts like" or "you reap what you sow". It states that everything we do, think, and feel gives off an energy vibration which attracts similar energy, just like two magnets attracted to each other. Everyone is living the Law of Attraction. Like it or not, we attract certain situations or people into our lives because of the energy we "put out there".

You can notice examples of the Law of Attraction in your life today.

- How many times does the phone ring and it is a friend that you were just thinking about?
- Have you ever talked about a particular loved one that has "transitioned" (passed away) and then you immediately see, hear, or smell something that reminds you of them?
- Have you ever seen someone that makes money hand over fist? The saying, "The rich get richer and the poor get poorer" is based on the Law of Attraction.
- Have you ever run into someone you were just thinking about but hadn't seen in years?
- Did you ever notice that the people who say, "I just can't catch a break" never do and the people that say "This will all work out" always seem to have things work out?

It is not our intent to reinvent the wheel and discuss the Law of Attraction in depth, but once you have a very basic understanding of the Law of Attraction, you can put it to work for you!

Exercise #1: Use the Law of Attraction in Your Day to Day Life

1. <u>Ask</u> – want, wish or set a clear goal!
   You have a legion of guides and loved ones (in both physical and non physical form) that are just waiting to assist you — you just have to ask. Set the intention, ask for guidance and assistance, and allow your dreams to manifest!

2. <u>Create the space</u>
   Take an action toward the desire, even if it is just a visualization or affirmation. Be clear and consistent and only affirm that which you truly desire.

3. <u>Allow the manifestation</u>
   Have faith! It can happen! But it might not happen in the manner that you expect - be open to the possibilities!

4. <u>Manifestation</u>
   This will come when your energetic vibration is in alignment with your desire.

Your job is to create your desired outcome through positive, consistent energy in alignment with your goal. You define the "what". It is the universe's job (universe can be defined as angels, God, spirit guides, or any other word that defines your personal belief system) to define "how" it will occur. It often won't occur as you expect.

This all sounds so easy, doesn't it? It really is, if you can get out of your own way.

We are not suggesting that you don't live in reality. Just gently guide your thoughts and actions toward that which you desire, hold the faith that source can deliver, and allow it to manifest with divine timing. Do not worry or think about all the possible negative outcomes that may occur. You do not want to give off any negative energy (worry, fear or guilt) as the universe does not evaluate the negativity or positivity of the energy that you project, it just delivers. If you are sending out a negative emotion, a negative outcome is what you will create. If you are sending out a positive emotion, a positive outcome is what you will create. It is your choice.

Many people think that their emotions or reactions are beyond their control…as if they are just somehow placed within their brain in response to factual occurrences in the world. In reality, those emotions and reactions occur as a result of how *you chose* to process your thoughts. They are a result of the story you tell yourself. Happiness (or any other feeling) is a CHOICE you make - not something that is or is not granted to you by unseen forces or circumstances. If "you can't catch a break", maybe it isn't because the world is conspiring against you, maybe you need to create a bigger catcher's mitt!

Ever notice how two people can experience the exact same circumstances, but walk away with vastly different interpretations? Your interpretations are a direct reflection of the way you process any given situation. They are not necessarily based upon hard facts, but instead may be influenced by your past experiences, your ego, and your emotional attachments. Remember that the way you *choose* to interpret a situation will have ramifications. The energy you create contributes to what your actual future experience will be through the Law of Attraction.

Finally, patience is key. As humans we see time as a very specific and valued commodity, and we want things NOW (or maybe even yesterday!). Remember the universe doesn't work on our schedule. What seems like a lifetime to us may be two minutes to those not in physical form.

Exercise #2: Mindful Observation

Through careful (non judgmental) observation, you can create your future experiences. Be aware of your feelings and remind yourself that your emotions occur as a result of your thoughts. If you catch yourself heading down a path of negativity or anything that is less than perfect for you, you can gently guide your thoughts into another direction. Don't freak out and start berating yourself for doing it "wrong", just tenderly guide your thoughts in a more positive direction. Your creation will manifest when your vibration is a match to your desire.

Watch for common pitfalls:

- Do you ever tell yourself you are screwing something up?
- Do you ever hear that inside voice say that you are an idiot or too slow, fast, tall, short, heavy, overwhelmed…whatever the criticism of the day is?
- Do you tell yourself you will never get something

done; you will never be happy; you will never be financially secure?
- Do you say your boss, spouse, friend is a "jerk" or any other negative word - maybe that is the quickest way to create that????
- Do you immediately judge something as bad or good or positive or negative -maybe it doesn't need to be labeled?

If you want to change your life in a positive direction, shift your thoughts, emotions, desires to be that of a more positive nature as well. You have the ability to create that which you focus on. Do you want to focus on worry, disease, the challenging or fearful aspects of life? Or, do you want to focus on perfect health, harmony, and well being? The choice is yours.

Try to become more observant of your thought patterns. We tell ourselves the same stories over and over again. If you really pay attention you will see repeated themes and patterns to your thoughts. How often do you drift back to an unresolved issue in your life and feed it energy? Even as you go about your normal day to day activities, compassionately observe your thought patterns. Do not allow this practice to be one which creates self judgment or doubt. We may find ourselves drifting into worry or negativity, but that is ok. Just gently guide yourself back to that place where you wish to be and remind yourself that this is a state of *becoming* what you want…not expecting it of ourselves overnight!

Exercise #3: Creating for Others

Once people learn to utilize the Law of Attraction to improve their lives, they will often want to help others with their new found experiences. But, can you create for another?

The quick answer - No, you cannot create for another individual. But, you can offer them positive energy in the form of sending loving thoughts or prayers. Positive energy or intentions cannot be forced upon another much like one who is suffering with addiction cannot be forced into rehabilitation programs. However, prayers don't have expiration dates. Those "good vibrations" can hang out and be activated once that individual is in a place that they can receive such positive energy. Once that person is in alignment with that healing vibration, your prayer (even if from long ago) will assist with creation.

So an exercise may be to set aside a time each day or each week to send out some healing thoughts or prayers for those in need. Do so without attachment to outcome but with the intent of surrounding them with love and support on whatever their personal journey is.

Exercise #4: Positive Affirmations

As a yoga teacher, Kim often suggests to send out healing thoughts and prayers as mentioned in previous exercises. However, when encouraging her students to project those same loving thoughts or prayers for themselves, she notices much more resistance. Maybe we need to learn to do for ourselves that which we can easily do for others.

Incorporating a daily practice of a positive affirmation can be very healing and helpful. Now, you don't have to look in the mirror and quote silly statements like the Stuart Smalley character from "Saturday Night Live", but you can find a daily affirmation that speaks to you. It must be heartfelt and sincere and setting aside a few moments each day for a positive affirmation is a good first step!

Below are samples of positive affirmations you may choose - or use your own! These were received by Lisa during various channeling sessions through the years.

- "I am worthy and able to receive abundance"

- "This life is perfect for me at this time, but I will make it even better now"

- "I am living and prospering in harmony"

- "I find nothing out of the ordinary, except the emotion of exuberant loving energy that runs through me!"

- Or make up your own….

Exercise #5: Journaling—the Quick and Easy Way!

Positive affirmations and intentions can take the written form too. Try this simple practice. Take a simple notebook that you may already have in your home.

Dr. Kimberly K. Friedman and Lisa Miliaresis

Everyday take 1 minute—just 1 minute—to write down 3 things…

I am grateful for _____ today.
I am _____.
I want _____.

They can be one word answers—they may be the same answers each day or different answers each day. It will just take a minute---but its creative potential is powerful!!

Chapter 4

Maintenance

Meditate to be clean and bright so you know what feels right. Follow your inner GPS and make your day the best of the best!
- Lisa Miliaresis via meditation 06-02-11

We are more than a physical body! So often in our culture we adopt our outward appearance as our identity. We forget that we are really spiritual beings; spiritual beings that temporarily inhabit a physical body in order to have a human learning experience. If we use only our physical senses, we can see, hear, touch and feel our bodies. But, if we use our non-physical senses, we can discover much more!

The non physical body is sometimes referred to as a spirit body, an energetic body, an auric body, a mental body, a biomagnetic electric field, etc. The label isn't important, but the realization that YOU ARE MORE THAN A PHYSICAL BODY is the important thing to understand. It is the interaction between our physical and non physical matter that creates our experiences on this Earth and allows us to live our individual journeys in joy and harmony.

So how do we keep our body(s) working in health and at peak potential? We are taught at a young age to take care of our physical bodies - shower, brush your hair, floss your teeth, eat a healthy diet, exercise, etc. But, were you ever taught to maintain your non-physical body(s)?

Just as our physical body can get "dirty", so can our energetic body. Energy is contagious! We can pick up energetic traces from our environment. Have you ever walked into a testing situation and felt the anxiety? Have you ever walked into a room filled with laughter and smiled without even knowing why? Have you ever felt the tension in a hospital setting? Just like we can catch a cold virus that affects our physical body, we can also "catch" things that affect our energetic body. We all know people that just drain us merely by their physical presence. It is as if they are "energy vampires" that can just suck the energy right out of you, often without even knowing what they are doing.

If you neglect to maintain your energy body, you may experience fatigue, illness, or pick up the energy of others that really isn't yours. Fortunately, there are many energy cleaning practices. We often say, "You have many tools in your toolbox". Your task is to find the practice or tools which appeal to you and work them into your daily routine just like brushing your teeth or combing your hair. Although it takes some practice, this ritual of cleaning your energy body just as you do your physical body can improve your life experience and deepen your sense of awareness and inner peace.

Energy Cleaning Tool Box - Exercises #1-12

Before you begin any of these exercises, just take a few deep breaths and check in…

- How do you feel?
- How is your energy?
- What is your vibration at this moment?
- Just notice without judgment or labels.

We will ask you these same questions after you practice these exercises. Know that it isn't about following each and every one, but picking and choosing which practices resonate with you. You might choose different tools for different days or different circumstances.

1. Prayer is an easy way to clean and clear energy. It doesn't have to conform to any particular ritual or time; you can send out prayers as you are sitting in traffic, working or exercising. So many times in Channeling sessions, Lisa will remind people to "just ask". It is as simple as asking through prayers or thoughts, silent or out loud.
Visualization and imagination can assist prayer as well. You might use the visualization of a white light surrounding and supporting you as you pray. This light is healing and full of the highest vibration of pure love. As you practice your prayers, know that no harm can come to you for you are protected and loved by this pure spiritual light. Visualize this light all around you, or feel

its warmth radiating through your body, or feel its vibration - use any or all of your senses as one particular sense might be easier for you than others. Another option is to visualize a paint brush or angel's wings just gently brushing away anything that is less than completely peaceful and in perfect harmony with your highest intentions.

2. Take a walk in nature – Whatever is available to you (beach, woods, park or just in front of your home) as you take each step, appreciate your surroundings. See if you can kick off your shoes and feel the energy of the earth below your feet. Maybe place your hands on the bark of a tree and feel the energy of that tree. Look at the plants, animals and just appreciate every step and breathe. Understand that we are so intimately connected with the cleansing energy of nature.

3. Sunlight and/or moonlight – Take a few minutes to be outside in the light of the sun or moon and feel the power of the universal love as it shines upon you. As silly as it may seem, ask the power of the moonlight or sunlight to clear any debris and to provide to its most healing vibration.

4. Smell lavender – You can grow a small pot in your home. You can even utilize the healing powers of lavender essential oils (or other extracts) and inhale the fragrances.

5. Burn sage – This is a nice way to clear any negative energy. You can grow your own sage or purchase it at many organic grocery stores or new age shops. (Use discretion as it does smell like marijuana.)

6. Another tool in the toolbox can be to associate energy cleaning with physical cleaning. Imagine as you shower you are cleaning both your energy and your physical body; all dirt and negativity will go down the drain never to harm another again. When you are done showering, you can pour some imaginary cleaner down the drain to permanently swoosh away anything that no longer serves you. No one will know that you are pouring imaginary energy "draino" down the drain-and you may even get a little chuckle out of it yourself.
7. Play with a pet. The unconditional love provided by a dog, cat or any pet can bring you from a negative vibration to a place of balance and harmony very quickly.
8. Crystals – each one has a vibration and level of healing. There are many good books on crystals and many workshops or internet courses on the different types of crystals. Or, you can just go by your instinct and select crystals that just speak to you without fully understanding the science behind the various types. You will often find both Kim and Lisa with crystals in their pockets.
9. MEDITATION, MEDITATION, MEDITATION – try a guided meditation like the one we have posted at www.2communicate.net. There are also meditation CD's available from book stores and you can find many good meditation resources from the internet. If a group setting is better, try a local yoga center as many offer meditation classes.

10. Try Yoga, Tai Chi, QiGong, and other physical practices that enhance your energy awareness and assist in clearing energy blockages.
11. Try Reiki, Healing Touch, acupuncture, or the assistance of energy healing practitioners that can assist you in cleansing and clearing your energy fields.
12. There are many books and tools available throughout various religious or spiritual practices. One which we find helpful is the practice of ho'oponopono which will be explained further in the next chapter.

After you have done any of these exercises, just take a few deep breaths and check in…

- How do you feel?
- How is your energy?
- What is your vibration at this moment?
- Just notice without judgment or labels.

Chapter 5

Balance

Act calmly, not coldly. Peace is greater than anger. Tranquility and harmony are the true order of things.
　　　　　　　　- Lao Tzu, The Tao Te Ching, 2500 BC

How do you maintain a steady vibration when the world around you is spinning? To maintain balance, we must ride the wave of life's journey; we could maybe call it "journey surfing". When the surf gets rough, you need to reach down deep into your tool box until you find the tools which allow you to find your neutral vibration - your place of balance and peace. Many spiritual teachers will use different labels or descriptions for this neutral vibration – feeling connected, going back to zero, shavasana, being present, internalizing, going deep within, finding zen, turning off the outside world, connecting with the loving and peaceful energy within, etc. As we have stated before, the label or terminology doesn't matter. The ability to remain calm, focused, connected to your place of intuition while remaining aware of your true identity as a spiritual being is what matters.

At times things seem to be very complex or difficult in our Earthly lives. In reality, our issues usually stem from something very simple - a fear, a judgment, a repeated pattern, etc. We need to compassionately catch ourselves as we fall into a negative thought process and resist the temptation to cover up our difficulties with busy work or self-created drama or alcohol or food or drugs. Allow yourself to feel and experience that loss of balance; it is there to teach you. Forgive yourself, release and clean your energy fields using your maintenance tools, breathe, and discover what is causing your loss of balance at its deepest roots.

One thing to keep in mind is that we tend to make everything more complicated by focusing on our problems instead of our solutions. We magnify what is wrong and ignore what is right. Remember the Law of Attraction? By focusing on what you don't want, by worrying about your problems, by fighting and forcing against that which is beyond your control; you are reinforcing exactly what you don't want to reinforce! The Law of Attraction does not know the words "don't want", it just feels the energy pull and sets about creating it. When you have a dislike, do not feed it energy. There is no need to nourish the negative vibe - counter it instead with a positive one. Don't waste your energy focusing on running away from an uncomfortable situation. Instead focus on running toward that which you desire.

Don't forget to ask! If you are stuck in an energetic place which is not comfortable for you, use meditation or prayer to ask for direction from your guides or angels or your own intuition. This can assist you in finding a positive path. The answers will come in different ways - through your dreams, daydreams, random thinking or you might just "know" the answer as you let go. Subtle messages tend to create clarity and balance if you can turn off the drama long enough to listen.

Obviously life will throw challenges your way. You wouldn't have bothered to come to this planet if you were going to coast through without any tough lessons. It is completely normal to feel overwhelmed or off balance at times. It is normal to catch yourself being short tempered or forgetting that you are more than just the roles and responsibilities you have in your Earthly life. The key is to catch those moments when they occur and gently guide yourself back to center, without judgment.

So what do you do when you find yourself "off balance"? First, be grateful that your compassionate observer was able to identify the imbalance. That is half the battle! Once you can honestly, non-judgmentally observe your own patterns without having to externally blame someone or something else, you will be able to restore your sense of harmony much more easily. In fact, sometimes it is often just observation and awareness alone that will create the release. Here are a few other suggestions:

- DO NOT ATTACH TO DRAMA. – If possible leave the room or ignore the drama. If you can't ignore the situation, we advise you to listen from a place of non-judgment. If you need to take action, evaluate from a neutral place and look at the situation from a broader perspective. Remember that we all evaluate situations through the lens of our own filters and previous experiences. Two people can experience the exact same circumstances and walk away with entirely different interpretations. The facts are the facts, but the story we tell ourselves about those facts can vary greatly. You are SURE of your interpretation and another person can be just as SURE about theirs, and yet your ideas can be complete polar opposites. Is digging your heels in and attaching to the drama of your particular story really helpful?

- STAY NON-JUDGMENTAL & NEUTRAL.– Use a tool from your tool box. The goal is to observe objectively without any attachment to any particular outcome. Many spiritual philosophies teach us that nothing is permanent and that things are often beyond our control. The human tendency toward the illusion that things are always within our control and must always be "fair" is very often the source of heartache and drama itself. Don't jump on the bandwagon or join the drama. Doing so will feed that energy and contribute to an energetic snowball effect.
- SEND UNCONDITIONAL LOVE TO YOURSELF AND TO OTHERS – Try to send out positive thoughts or prayers to all involved, even those with whom you may disagree.
- DO UNTO OTHERS - Most of us were taught to be courteous to one another. In most religions there is some form of the Golden Rule - Do unto others as you would have them do unto you. In a perfect world it would be nice if we could always

practice that tenet, but we can maintain balance by striving for that ideal.

- HO'OPONOPONO or similar practices - Ho'oponopono is an ancient Hawaiian practice of reconciliation and forgiveness. This practice clears stuck energy with the use of a simple mind tools and a main mantra of "I love you. I am sorry. Please forgive me. Thank you!" Although we do not teach this practice, there are many terrific teachers and workshops and books that can provide additional insight into this practice. For the purpose of this book, we will explain how we understand and use this practice, but if you are interested in learning more about Ho'oponopono please go to this website http://www.self-i-dentity-through-hooponopono.com where you can seek out seminars affiliated with Ihaleakala Hew Len, PhD.

In our utilization of Ho'oponopono, we believe everything in our life is something we have attracted knowingly or unknowingly. Therefore, we are 100% responsible for what shows up in our lives. We are to utilize our experiences for growth, learning, and understanding and it is our duty to clear the stuck energy within us with the assistance from the divine and the use of the Ho'oponopono mantra. Look at the words in the mantra. They are extremely powerful in their meaning and in their vibration:

I love you - unconditional love for myself and others. (Self love is a very important component.)

I am sorry – asking for forgiveness for whatever I have created, knowingly or unknowingly, in this lifetime or maybe even from the beginning of time. I don't need to understand or analyze it; I am just sorry for those things that I may have done that are not in alignment with my higher spiritual intent.

Please forgive me - petition of forgiveness for those things mentioned above.

Thank you – have faith and believe that the divine (God, spirit, angels, guides, universe, whatever word you choose) has heard and will forgive and release this stuck energy.

Chapter 6

Nourish Yourself

Our food should be our medicine and our medicine should be our food.

- Hippocrates, Greek physician
(460 BC - 377 BC)

The dictionary defines the word nourish as "to provide with food or other substances necessary for life and growth". Although commonly used in reference to food, nourishment does not necessarily apply to only one aspect of our existence. As previously discussed, we consist of multiple "bodies" if you will; the physical body, the energetic body, the mental or thought body, and the spiritual body. If any one part or layer of our existence falls into a state of malnourishment, our entire being will become off-balance or suffer in some way. It is within the healthy union of all of our "bodies" that we will find the most harmony and peace.

In examining our relationship with the physical body, we have all heard about the importance of a healthy diet and exercise. Yet, we live in a culture where the obesity rate skyrockets each year and where children have a shorter life expectancy than their parents for the first time in history. We try to force ourselves into the latest diet craze or we strain our bodies into fetes of strength or flexibility that are beyond our current means - all in the quest for that perfect magazine cover body. And even when we find ourselves living with a healthy diet and exercise balance, is our motivation coming from a desire to be healthy or coming from a place of creating that perfect external appearance?

In the ancient Sanskrit language there is a term **ahimsa** and it means to do no harm or violence. It is often applied in teachings to illustrate the desire to do no harm to others, to nature, to animals, to the environment, etc. But, can the teaching of ahimsa also be applied to self? Is it healthy for you to conform to the latest diet fast or to force yourself into a physical exercise program that is not in alignment with your physical body?

Some people feel as though a vegetarian diet, or a vegan diet, or a macrobiotic diet, or a meat rich diet, or some other diet is the ultimate best diet for all. And for each diet plan you will find expert after expert, book after book, touting why it's better than every other diet available. How do you know what is really right for you? The same can be said of exercise plans…jazzercise or yoga or pilates or isometrics or pumping iron or aerobics or Latin dance…is there really one perfect exercise plan for all?

One of the main intents of this workbook is to enhance your ability to listen to your inner voice. Listening to your gut instinct or intuition can also be applied to nourishing your physical body. While a vegetarian diet might be ideal for some, it might not be ideal for everyone. Although competing in a triathlon may be for some, it may not be for you. More importantly, there is no reason to judge yourself should you not be comfortable with the diet or exercise routine that is being held up by some expert to be one of superiority. Does trying to follow someone else's rulebook of what diet and exercise should be for you really adhere to the intent of ahimsa? If you're truly going to be nonviolent in nature, you must be nonviolent to yourself as well. Violence does not have to be in the literal sense of violence, but could be more figurative in terms of forcing yourself to do something that is not in alignment with your inner being or judging yourself as "less than" because you are not conforming to the societal standard of the day.

Does that mean that ice cream can now become the meal of choice for everyday? Of course not. However, maybe you can treat yourself to ice cream, or whatever your favorite treat is, occasionally. The key is moderation. The important thing to remember is that nourishing your body is connected to nourishing your energy, your spirit, and your mind. If you are being forceful or violent in the way in which you structure your diet and exercise routine, is that force or energy also feeding your overall being? Taking a softer and gentler approach with your physical being will often allow you to find that you naturally eat and behave in a healthier manner. Incorporating balance, variety, and moderation may just naturally become a byproduct of being driven by the internal light within you. Access your own internal rulebook; observe what makes you feel better.

But, it isn't just about our physical body. Remember that the energy of the food you consume can create energetic ripples for the rest of your body. When you become mindful and understand that "you are what you eat", you will find yourself slowly drifting into a healthier eating pattern – not because it is forced, not because someone told you that it is the miracle diet to follow – but because it is the diet that feels right and nourishes your body and soul.

The same can be applied to exercise. Ahimsa in exercise means not forcing or causing physical harm. If you're going to the gym or an exercise class out of some obligation, is that really creating the energy that you want for your physical body? Instead, can you go to the gym because you want your body to function at its most healthful pace? Can you find gratitude for the abilities and functions of your beautiful physical body and want to enhance that through exercise? Obligation or Gratitude-either of those options looks exactly the same on the outside, but internally and energetically there is a world of difference! Which energy do you want to feed yourself?

Exercise #1: Mindful Eating

For this exercise you will need a small item of food like a raisin, a grape, a nut, a small piece of cheese or some other small food item that you can completely contain in your mouth in one bite. For the purposes of this workbook we will use a raisin, but you could substitute any food that works for you.

Take the raisin in your hand. Notice the texture. Feel the ridges, the bumps, the areas that are more smooth, or the areas that have a rougher texture beneath your fingers. Feel the weight of the raisin in your hand. Notice the temperature of the raisin. Now, notice the appearance of the raisin. Take your time. Study the ridges, the color, the size, its overall appearance. Slowly bring the raisin up to your nose and inhale the fragrance. Does it have any subtle scent? Now when you have explored the raisin fully with your sense of sight and touch and smell, gently place the raisin on the tip of your tongue and close your mouth. Notice the texture of the raisin against your tongue. Move the raisin around. Draw little circles with your tongue letting the raisin just tumble within your mouth. Allow the raisin to go to the inside of the cheeks. Gently grasp the raisin between your teeth, but don't bite down quite yet. Notice if there's any sense of taste before you even bite. Finally, allow yourself to gently bite into the raisin. Fully experience the taste. Notice if it is salty or sweet or sour or something else. Is there any sound that you make as you chew the raisin? Notice the feel of any saliva in your mouth or the temperature in your mouth. Take a moment to give thanks to the Earth, the sun, the water which help to support the growth of this grape that later became a raisin. Continue to chew much longer than you might normally chew. Notice each time the teeth come back into contact and then again as they separate. And then when you have fully experienced the entirety of eating the raisin, allow it to gently move to the back of the mouth cavity and swallow. Notice how it feels as the raisin moves down your throat. Notice any taste that lingers in your mouth.

Can you imagine if we ate each meal with such sensitivity and observation? Would we still tend to overindulge if we ate with such mindfulness? Would we become more aware of the quiet impulses that inform us when we are no longer hungry? Although this mindful eating exercise would certainly be extreme if we were to do this with everything that we ate, if we take the time to become slightly more mindful maybe we would make choices that were more healthy and supportive for our bodies.

One word of caution about nourishing the physical body: we have noticed that some people who choose to follow a spiritual path feel that it is necessary to transcend or "rise above" those things that are of a physical nature. If it is a part of your personal path to fast or abstain from various physical activities, then that is fine for you and you should embrace that path. However, we personally don't believe that it is necessary to shun the physical nature of our being in order to obtain spiritual growth. In our view, it is important to find a healthy balance between enjoying those things of physical nature with those things of a spiritual nature. We do not believe that we chose to manifest into a physical form for the purposes of abstaining from experiences that are both physical and spiritual in nature. We are here to learn, and that includes lessons of the body.

One other thing to consider - does the forceful straining to avoid a temptation actually cause the attachment to that very temptation? Remember back to the last time that you were on a diet. How many times did you think about the exact foods that you weren't allowed to have? Maybe instead of focusing on what you can't have, maybe it's time to focus on the positive of what you can have. Maybe the key doesn't lie in trying to resist those things that bring enjoyment to the physical body, but instead to practice moderation and balance.

Moderation and Balance - how many times do we hear those words? But how do we really apply that in the real world? If you thoroughly enjoy chocolate cake, allow yourself to experience it occasionally. Maybe even enjoy a bite of chocolate cake using the mindful meditation exercise from earlier in this chapter: it will be the best bite of chocolate cake you have ever had! However, if you allow your entire diet to consist of chocolate cake, your physical body will not function at its peak potential and it will interfere with your ability to fully experience your life. As another example, if you were to become consumed with weight lifting, you would quickly lose flexibility within your physical body. Conversely, if you neglect to do anything of a weight-bearing nature, your muscles will become weak and your bones will become brittle.

The same principles apply to all of the layers or bodies of our existence. Physically the nourishment of food is obvious. Mentally, study after study has shown the importance of keeping the mind active. Senior citizens are often encouraged to perform mental activities like crossword puzzles in order to keep their minds sharp. Energetically, we nourish our body by employing some of the tools in our toolbox which were previously discussed in other chapters. Spiritually, we nourish ourselves with whatever spiritual or religious practices speak to you. It is within the balance of nourishing the physical, mental, energetic, spiritual bodies that we find most join in harmony in our lives.

Exercise #2: Nourish the Physical

Try something new today. Take a yoga class. Maybe try Tai chi. How about lifting weights. Maybe go for a brisk walk. What form of physical movement feels right for you today? Honor your physical body. Stay within your limitations. But don't be afraid to set a realistic personal goal for yourself and nourish your body. Experiment and try different forms of physical exercise. Find what works for you. And know that what works for you one day may not be the same the next. Whatever you do, do it with the knowledge that you are giving your body the gift of health just as you have been granted the gift of this body which allows you to learn and protects you during your time on this planet.

Exercise #3: Nourish the Physical (2)

Try something else new today. Is there a fruit or vegetable you've always seen at the store and you've wondered what it is? Can you combine exercise number two and number three and actually walk to a farmers market or road side stand to try a new produce item? Explore and open yourself to the unknown. And don't forget that if you are able to eat in a very healthy manner, feel free to grant yourself a small treat or reward so that you don't feel deprived in any way.

Exercise #4: Nourish the Mind

Try a new puzzle book. Or maybe download the latest word game onto your cell phone. Maybe there's a book that you've always wanted to read that you just couldn't give yourself the time or permission to read. Find some new mental challenge. Have you looked into community classes at the local community college or high school? Maybe watch an educational video on line. Have you checked out TED online? It is a compilation of videos with the sub tag: Ideas worth spreading.

Exercise #5: Nourish the Energy and Spirit

You are reading this book - that's good start. Can you also find 5 minutes – just 5 minutes – for meditation today? We take the time to charge our cell phone batteries; we also need to take the time to charge our internal batteries. Go to www.2communicate.net to try a quick guided meditation. Some meditations can be just a few minutes. Why not try it?

Trying to follow the conventional externally driven ideal or some notion of what is appropriate may not be in alignment with your personal internal compass. LISTEN and LEARN and we will discover what will allow us to function in the most harmonious way. Our body has innate wisdom. Sometimes we just choose not to listen.

- If we listen, we won't overeat.
- If we listen, we will move when our body feels sluggish.
- If we listen, we will energize our bodies with sunlight and nature.
- If we listen, we will challenge our minds when they become stagnant.
- If we listen, we will pull tools from our toolbox when we find ourselves feeling down or depressed.
- If we listen, we will find a deeper connection to our inner wisdom, our spirit guides, and that universal energy which is available to support us at all times.

Listening leads to nourishing. If we just listen...

Chapter 7

Ethics

All persons ought to endeavor to follow what is right, and not what is established.
- Aristotle, Greek philosopher
(384 BC-322 BC)

Ahhh, the beauty and wonders of being human! We *want* to only act from the highest of intentions for the good of all, but we still have our defense mechanisms, personalities, and human nature. We can sometimes be driven by the need to feel special or "better than". We have a human ego that likes to insert judgments, compare to others or interfere with our connection to higher guidance. Sometimes we have to take a deep breath, pause, and really look in the mirror. Are we really operating from a place of peace and love, or is there a bit of ego at play?

There is the source of divine love and light within each one of us. As we become more in touch with our inner spirituality, we will find that our intuition is heightened. Others may even begin to seek out our guidance or insight. However, we need to really consider whether our counsel is coming from our higher spiritual self, or coming from our mind's attempt to elevate oneself or manipulate others. It is an easy trap to fall into, even for those that we may consider "masters" or "experts". This is where ethics comes in.

Ethics is a set of principles or right conduct. It is a theory of moral values and an understanding between you and your inner being. As you learn to elevate your energy and spiritual connection, you must also learn to recognize when your ego starts to play a part in your motivations. Once recognized, you can gently clear away that which isn't serving your higher purpose so you can function from a place of love and light.

Ego can come to you in many shapes & sizes. As Lisa was developing her abilities as a medium, she often had to decipher whether the messages she was receiving were truly that of spirit or whether they were a creation of her own mind or ego. As you can imagine, if people are traveling great distances to see you in workshops and praising your abilities to communicate with those who have crossed over, it could be easy to slip into a place of believing that you are somehow special. Lisa had to develop the awareness that she provided a means of communication that could be very healing and helpful to others, but that these communications traveled through her without being about her.

So how does Lisa know if a message is ego or spirit? If the message comes in a way of fear or does not feel positive, she knows that it is not a message from higher intentions and she quickly diffuses it. That doesn't mean that spirits don't come to her with their personalities and that those personalities don't sometimes contain vibrations of anger. She will sometimes receive valid communications from those who are expressing something that we might consider unpleasant. However, that unpleasant discussion might be exactly what needs to take place in order for healing to occur and it comes wrapped up with the higher intention of love and peace. It *feels* different than a message that seems to come from ego.

The way to diffuse thoughts or messages that seem to be hurtful in intent is to recognize and acknowledge it as ego. Once you have the understanding that your thought is really coming from a place of trying to make you feel better about yourself, feel more important, or to satisfy some personal need; then you can compassionately dismiss it. Remember that it is normal for your ego to attempt to make things about you – that is the ego's job. However, if you catch yourself in a place of inserting your own personal needs and biases into messages of a higher nature, it is time to recognize that and release it. Don't get too upset with yourself; just laugh, notice, and move on.

Lisa begins each channeling session with a prayer that asks for assistance in delivering messages only from the higher good and only from those coming from light and love. If she needs extra assistance in diffusing a negative vibe, she will take a few deep breaths and ask Archangel Michael to assist her. Through meditation and channeling, we have received many lessons and messages of a higher vibration which have always been a product of pure love, and sincerity. **True inspiration is never hurtful in message or intent.**

The following experiences helped Lisa to develop her personal ethical standard as a medium:

Experience #1 (in Lisa's words)

- ❖ I heard a buzzing noise in my ear and awoke to see this beautiful angelic image. I think it was female with very short hair and delicate features. She was floating closer to me but was only visible from her waist up surrounded by a white mist. My heart was beating a mile a minute, and I dare not speak because I was so excited. I did not want her to leave without explaining why she was there. She spoke to me telepathically and said, "Don't be afraid". I could not help it, my heart was still racing, but her vibration was so soft and calming that I settled the best I could. She said, "You're going to be used like a telephone." I could not keep my mind calm enough to just listen. Instead I began to silently ask about my life and my husband's health. She said, "You are not to know everything about yourself or you would ruin your sweet life." Then she proceeded to give me a protocol.
    1. Always tell the truth
    2. Don't be judgmental of others
    3. Be respectful

Experience #2 (from meditation)
May all of our communications result in: Love, Understanding & Respect:

- ❖ Love – is the easy part and, in many cases, unconditional
- ❖ Understanding – is the hard part and we must try to understand differences between beliefs, traditions, culture, events, lifestyles etc.
- ❖ Respect – once we understand that there are differences, we must respect one another

Experience #3 Are you ready? (in Lisa's words)
I had been receiving the same message for many, many days, "Are you ready?" In the early morning of February 9, 2008, I heard something different. This time the message was, "You are ready." I fell back asleep and awoke to the sound of a non-physical phone ringing. I somehow knew that this was a symbolic communication to go downstairs and meditate. Someone was "calling" me. It was then I received a message from Lao-tzu:

CODE OF HONOR

- *   Allow without pressure.
- *   Encourage without promise
- *   Believe without notice
- *   Achieve without push
- *   Allow with a breath & thought
- *   Love unconditionally
- *   These are our laws of attraction. This is your code

of honor. Work with this code & succeed with many miracles. We support you and your efforts. All totally encompassing. True Believers in You! Today! Now Love to All.

Lisa's interpretation:

* Allow without pressure - create and let it go. relax
* Encourage without promise – deliver messages without attachment to validation
* Believe without notice - have faith, you don't have to have proof to believe
* Achieve without push – creations manifest easier if you just let it go
* Allow with a breath & thought - relax
* Love unconditionally - <3

So with an understanding of ethics, what comes next? Whether you choose to utilize spiritual practices for your own personal growth or whether you chose to share spiritual practices with clients, you must consistently remind yourself to allow this work to flow through you with love and compassion and the highest of ethical standards. A few pointers:

- Understand that you are the vessel or means to bring this energy to your client and that it isn't really about you or your ego.
- Take caution to not become what we jokingly refer to as a "spiritual snob". Don't buy into the belief that one way is "better than" another as we all

possess our own gifts, and we are all on our own perfect spiritual path.
- Appearances can be deceiving. Remember that someone who appears to be a destitute bum living on the streets may in reality be someone who is so incredibly spiritually evolved that he chose this path for himself as a means of educating others about compassion.
- Don't attach to the outcome of your work. Set the intention that your work will do the highest good for you and others, but understand that we don't always know what that highest good is. Allow the work to flow through you.
- Don't forget that you must maintain your own personal body, mind, and spirit through your own personal practices before you can assist others.

Chapter 8

Connecting the Dots

A human being is a part of the whole called by us universe, a part limited in time and space. He experiences himself, his thoughts and feeling as something separated from the rest, a kind of optical delusion of his consciousness. This delusion is a kind of prison for us, restricting us to our personal desires and to affection for a few persons nearest to us. Our task must be to free ourselves from this prison by widening our circle of compassion to embrace all living creatures and the whole of nature in its beauty.

- Albert Einstein,
March 1879 – April 1955

The illusion of separateness....

- Why do we feel that we are so different than others?
- Why is my religion or tribe or belief system or ethnicity somehow better than yours?
- Why do I feel the need to sway or convert others over to my belief system?

- Why does our desire to validate that we are "better than" or "smarter than" or "right" become so necessary to our egos, and why does that lead to the need to prove someone else is "lesser than", "less intelligent" or "wrong"?
- When did the need to be evangelical with our belief systems shift into a place that it is ok to employ violence toward others in order to force cohesion of beliefs?
- Why if I accidentally cut someone off in traffic I can consider that a simple mistake. But, if someone else cuts me off in traffic, it requires a middle finger gesture or anger? Do I honestly think whoever pulled out in front of me woke up that morning and said, "Yippee, I get to cut someone off today!"?

Oh the wonderful silliness of human beings and our egos! We somehow interpret things through a filter that suggests that we are completely different than others. We are all just feeding our minds whatever story we tell ourselves to justify our actions or beliefs - your story is no better than mine.

We are all spiritual beings having a human experience. We are here to learn whatever lessons we have chosen for ourselves. And, we all are going about it with whatever tools we have in our own personal toolboxes. We really aren't that different; we just think we are!

We all want health, happiness, love, safety or some other form of freedom. During the day, we are kept busy in our routine of life, creating our own personal journeys.

Yet collectively we are really co-creating with our fellow beings on a local and global level. If there is a natural disaster on the other side of the planet, it may not affect our getting to and from work that day, but it does affect us. Where were you on September 11, 2001 and how did it affect you personally even if you didn't know a single person directly involved.

Obviously not each moment of every day will result in the power to collectively share an experience like those of September 11th, but that same concept occurs on a smaller level every moment of everyday. From a broader political perspective, you can easily see how opposing groups feed off one another. However, on an individual basis, you affect me and I affect you, and we both affect the experiences and circumstances we draw into our lives.

The intention of this book is to assist you with connecting to your inner being and higher self. However, in the process of becoming more aware of self, you will also develop an awareness of the associations we have to others. We are connected to nature, other individuals, our communities, our society, our country, our world, our dimension, and the next dimension. Everything in our experience has a vibration which holds a level of energy; whether it is a living being, plant, object, thought or emotion. And, these energies interact and affect our lives. Much of what we are is influenced by the people, the nature, and the emotions around us at all time; it is all interrelated!

By employing positive thought and energy elevating practices found throughout this book, your energy vibrates at a higher frequency and will affect the energy of those around you. There is a scientific principle called entrainment that applies here. Entrainment is defined as the tendency for two oscillating bodies to lock into phase so that they vibrate in harmony or the synchronization of two or more rhythmic cycles. Typical examples of entrainment are found throughout physics, biology, and chemistry. If you put several pendulum clocks together in a room, in time the pendulums will begin to sway in unison. When two individual heart muscles are brought close together, they begin pulsing in synchrony. Another example of the entrainment effect is women who live in the same household often find that their menstrual cycles begin to coincide. An object's or individual's energy patterns will influence the energetic patterns of others! A practice of positive vibration will create energetic ripples that will ultimately result in an overall energetic elevation around you! If you choose to spend your time with negative thought patterns or pessimism or critical judgments, you will watch your energy plummet. Conversely, spend your time with positive thoughts, people and circumstances; and you can soar!

Always remember the power of one; your individual vibration, energy, attitude or thought combines with those of others. This combination can be incredibly powerful, but it can't begin without you!

Through channeling, Lisa has learned that after the death of the physical body, a Guide will assist an individual with a life review. This review illustrates how one's actions have affected others during his/her time on Earth. The details of the particular action aren't the emphasis; the ripple effect of the action upon others is what is highlighted. Our judgments, words, thoughts and actions all hold energy, and it is what those judgments, words, thoughts, and actions set in motion that really matters! Think of it like rows and rows of stacked dominoes with multiple offshoots and interweaving pathways. Our domino, our initial action, topples the first domino and creates a wave of unknown consequences that we can't possibly see from our first domino position in the line. We can't be perfect, but we must always try to remember that the energy we put out into the universe will have consequences seen and unseen.

Let's try some exercises to enhance our awareness of our energetic influence in life.

Exercise #1: Breath of Appreciation

When you wake and take the first conscious breath of the day, take a moment to find at least one thing to appreciate. Focus on this appreciation and really relax into it. You may find yourself smiling. During the day as you embark upon life challenges, just stop for a second and remember that feeling of appreciation, or better yet, find something about the challenge to appreciate and take a few breaths to shift your vibration.

Exercise #2: Choose a Shift

Take notice of the space you occupy. Take notice of how you feel. Simply pay attention! Is the energy one of neutrality, happy, sad, angry or something else? Energy can be shifted if you choose to shift it and the first step is discovering what it is.

CHOOSE TO BE POSITIVE - Use a tool that you have learned - mediation, prayer, affirmation, or ho'oponopono- whichever one appeals to you. Often yoga or tai chi or chi gong or meditation will provide practice in just being present to the simple moments in your life so you can notice when the energy shifts to a place that is less than healthy and healing.

Exercise #3: Detach from Drama

The next time you find yourself in a situation where someone is creating "drama", do not attach to the experience of the drama. It is a bit of a balancing act! Try to stay supportive and positive, without feeding into the excited energy, adding to the judgments, or fanning the flames. If you stay calm and focused on positivity and love, you will witness a shift in the room and others.

Keep in mind, our life is a series of lessons for our soul's growth. It isn't about the day to day drama of life on earth; it is about the opportunities for learning that those dramas present to us. **The positive energy of one can be powerful and contagious. Be conscious of your vibration and create the experience and world we want to live in.** As Ghandi said, "Be the change you wish to see in the world."

Epilogue

"When you extend your goodwill in every direction, regardless of circumstances, you begin to see that we are all one."
                                     - Lao-Tzu, The Tao Te Ching, 2500 BC

Thank you for taking the time to go on this journey with us. We hope this book brings you some insight into what you are seeking and provides pathways toward finding it. Feel free to keep this workbook as a reference and play with the exercises as they call to you. You already possess many of the answers and tools within you - just use these practices to turn up the volume on your internal guidance system and trust the process.

    Many of these chapters came directly from questions asked by those who attend our various classes and workshops. Understandably, the same questions arise over and over again. It seems we all search for the same things in life: love, happiness, peace, security, and an everlasting connection to others. These things are available to us all if we can allow it to be so.

    We know that not every day will bring perfect positivity and enlightenment. We are concerned with overall progress toward harmony with compassion for those human missteps that are bound to occur. We obviously have to live in this world with all the trials that entails, and our goal is not to escape or avoid living! But, if we can see things from a higher perspective, we can find the hidden learning opportunities in the difficult times, find peace even in the midst of chaos, and set into motion energy that is uplifting and healing for ourselves and others. Along the way, you may even find that you begin to uncover abilities that were lying dormant until you opened a pathway for their expression.

For all of those who have found their way to this book - we love you, we're sorry, please forgive us, and thank you! We hope you maintain a connection to love and peace throughout this day, your lifetime, and beyond this lifetime! Namaste.

About the Authors

Lisa Miliaresis

Lisa is a psychic medium, speaker, and author. Born with the ability to channel, she instinctively followed her internal guidance and fine tuned her abilities until she became an accomplished medium with a lifetime of experiences. Her ability to bridge communications from those on the other side has helped many clients find comfort and healing. Her goals:

- Bring awareness of the eternal nature of life
- Encourage others to meditate and find their own Light Driven Guidance
- Assist others with understanding and respecting this wonderful form of communication

Lisa channels publicly in large seminars, small groups, and private individual sessions throughout the country. She has appeared in multiple radio broadcasts and newspaper articles, and you can read about Lisa's early journey in her book "Being Light Driven; Finding Inner Guidance". www.2communicate.net for more information.

Dr. Kimberly K Friedman

Kim is a Certified Past Life Regression Counselor (through the Academy for Professional Hypnosis Training) who assists clients in unlocking deep memories, releasing repeated patterns and discovering spiritual, physical and mental wellbeing. A lifelong student and teacher, Kim completed a traditional doctoral education as an optometric physician in addition to certifications as a registered yoga teacher and reiki master. She is a partner in an eye care practice in Moorestown, NJ, teaches yoga classes, and also works as an instructor for a yoga alliance certified teacher training program. Within the various roles she fulfills in her life, she has made multiple television appearances on such programs as the Rachael Ray Show, Fox's Good Day, Cn8's Your Morning, and Comcast Newsmakers. She also co-created spiritual based workshops to support charities.

CPSIA information can be obtained at www.ICGtesting.com
Printed in the USA
BVOW00s0336310713

327265BV00001BA/1/P